# Cuban Americans

TIFFANY PETERSON

Heinemann Library
Chicago, Illinois

© 2003 Heinemann Library
a division of Reed Elsevier Inc.
Chicago, Illinois

Customer Service 888-454-2279

Visit our website at www.heinemannlibrary.com

Created by the publishing team at Heinemann Library
Designed by Roslyn Broder
Photo research by Amor Montes de Oca
Printed and Bound in the United States by Lake Book Manufacturing, Inc.

07 06 05 04 03
10 9 8 7 6 5 4 3 2 1

**Library of Congress Cataloging-in-Publication Data**
Peterson, Tiffany, 1968-
  Cuban Americans / Tiffany Peterson.
     p. cm. -- (We are America)
Summary: Describes the conditions in Cuba that led people to
immigrate to the United States and what their daily lives are like
in their new home.
  Includes bibliographical references (p.  ) and index.
  ISBN 1-40340-733-9 (lib. bdg.) -- ISBN 1-40343-134-5 (pbk.)
  1.  Cuban Americans--Juvenile literature. 2.  Immigrants--United States--Juvenile Literature--3. United States--Emigration and immigration. 4. Cuba--Emigration and immigration--Juvenile literature. 5. Cuban Americans--Biography--Juvenile literature. 6. Immigrants--United States--Biography--Juvenile literature. [1. Cuban Americans.]  I. Title. II. Series.
  E184.C97P482003
  973'.04687291--dc21

                                    2002013097

**Acknowledgments**
The author and publishers are grateful to the following for permission to reproduce copyright material: pp. 4, 5 Corbis; pp. 7, 8, 10, 14, 19, 27 Historical Museum of Southern Florida; pp. 9, 13 Hulton Archive/Getty Images; pp. 11, 12 Bettmann/Corbis; p. 15 Tony Arruza/Corbis; p. 17 AP Wide World Photos; p. 18 Jacques Langeviu/AP Wide World Photos; p. 20 Hans Deryk/AP Wide World Photos; p. 21 Alan Diaz/AP Wide World Photos; p. 22 Michael Keller/Corbis; p. 23 A. J. C./Corbis; p. 24 Graeme Teague; p. 25 Jeff Greenberg/PhotoEdit, Inc.; p. 26 Jose Goita/AP Wide World Photos; p. 27 Joe Raedle/Getty Images; pp. 28, 29 Courtesy of Christopher Bello

Cover photograph by (foreground) Michael Keller/Corbis, (background) Historical Museum of South Florida

Special thanks to Mariela Ferretti of the Cuban American National Foundation and Jaime Suchlicki of the University of Miami's Institute for Cuban and Cuban-American Studies for their comments in preparation of this book. Tiffany Peterson thanks Jorge Castillo and icuban.com for their help and contributions.

Some quotations and material used in this book come from the following source. In some cases, quotes have been abridged for clarity: http://www.streamnologies.com/cc-peter-pan.htm

Some words are shown in bold, **like this.** You can find out what they mean by looking in the glossary.

To learn more about the Cuban-American family on the cover of this book, turn to page 22. A historic shot of a store in Little Havana, a Cuban-American neighborhood in Miami, Florida, is shown in the background.

# Contents

# Christopher's Story

In 1980, Cubans who wanted to leave Cuba had to ask the government for permission. Christopher Bello asked to go to the United States, where his father lived. His father rented a boat to go to Cuba and bring Christopher to Florida. On the day Christopher was supposed to leave, there were huge crowds of people in Mariel, Cuba, and many boats. He couldn't find his father, so he got on the nearest boat. He was not even sure the boat would go to the United States.

*This boat left Cuba from the same place that Christopher left—Mariel, Cuba. It was photographed near Florida on June 4, 1980.*

The small boat was heavy, because there were 27 people on it. As the boat got closer to Florida, it began to sink. The United States **Coast Guard** arrived just in time. All 27 people were rescued. In many ways, Christopher is a lot like many other Cuban Americans. He was willing to risk his life for a chance at freedom in the United States. According to him, that's something he could have never had in Cuba.

*This is a photo of the **refugee** center at Fort Chaffee, Arkansas, that Christopher was sent to after he was rescued. It shows a family from Cuba having a meal at the center.*

I slept those eighteen days [at Fort Chaffee] on the floor and my pillow was the plastic bag with the things that the **Red Cross** had given me.
—Christopher Bello

# Cuba

Cuba is a long, narrow island in the Caribbean Sea. It is very close to the United States. It is closest to the city of Key West, Florida. It is only 90 miles (145 kilometers) from Key West. In fact, the **climate** in Cuba is similar to that of Florida. The temperature ranges from 70°F (21°C) in January to about 80°F (27°C) in July.

*This map shows how close Cuba is to the state of Florida.*

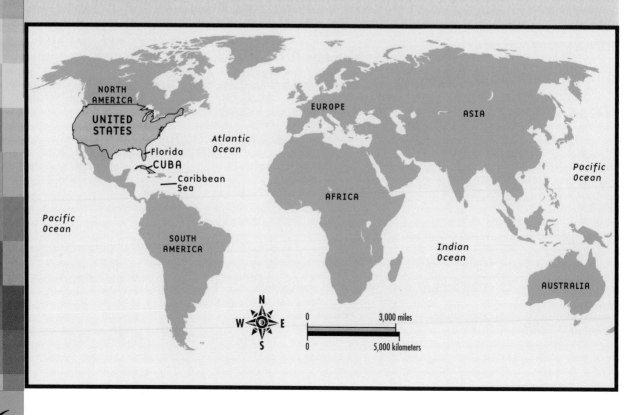

*Workers in Cuba are shown here standing on a train that is loaded with sugarcane, which is Cuba's most important crop.*

Cuba is known as one of the most beautiful islands in the Caribbean. It has many mountains and hills. It is also rich in **natural resources.** Its climate allows farmers to grow sugarcane and tobacco. The tobacco grown in Cuba is known around the world as being the best tobacco for cigars. Cigar rolling is a big Cuban **industry.**

Cuba has two distinct seasons. The rainy season runs from May to October, and the dry season runs from November to April.

# A Brief History of Cuba

Christopher Columbus landed in Cuba in 1492, and Spain quickly took control of the island. Cuba remained a Spanish **colony** for hundreds of years. Cubans tried several times to break free from Spanish rule. In 1898, the United States decided to help Cuba. Future U.S. president Teddy Roosevelt and soldiers known as the Rough Riders went to Cuba to fight against the Spanish soldiers. In July 1898, the United States defeated Spain, and Cuba was freed.

*The war in which U.S. soldiers, shown below, fought Spanish forces in Cuba became known as the Spanish-American War.*

*Fidel Castro worked for years training his army to help him take over power in Cuba. He is in the center of this photo taken in 1959.*

Cuba was free from Spain, but it had to rely on the United States for money and business. Fidel Castro changed that. In 1959, he and his **guerrilla** army took power in Cuba. Castro became the leader of Cuba, and Cuba became a **communist** country. He still ruled Cuba in 2003. Many people think he is a **dictator.**

# The First Cuban Immigrants

When Cuba was still a Spanish **colony**, the first Cubans came to the United States. Beginning in the 1830s, cigar rollers came to Florida. They **settled** in Key West and Tampa in Florida. In 1866, some Cuban cigar companies moved their factories to Florida. They moved because there was a war in Cuba. Many of the tobacco fields had been burned. Many Cuban workers went to Florida to work in the cigar factories.

*While Cuban cigar rollers worked, they sometimes listened to a person hired to read aloud from newspapers and books.*

*This picture, taken April 15, 1933, shows Cuban Americans who were angry about the rule of Gerardo Machado. Machado had been elected president of Cuba in 1925. He turned out to be a dishonest leader.*

The Cubans who stayed in the United States created Cuban-American communities in Florida and New York. They kept in touch with their friends and families in Cuba. They created newspapers in the United States that told about events in Cuba. When Fulgencio Batista took over as the leader of Cuba in 1933, Cuban Americans knew all about it. They also knew about Fidel Castro forcing Batista out of power in 1959.

# Escaping Castro's Cuba

When Fidel Castro took control of Cuba in 1959, he turned Cuba into a **communist** country. The government took over businesses and limited the amount of land a person could own. People were no longer allowed to follow their religious beliefs. Many Cubans left Cuba by taking flights to Florida until 1973. The flights were known as the Freedom Flights.

In 1961, the United States government helped a group of Cuban Americans go to Cuba to try to overthrow Castro. They were not successful. As a result, Castro wanted to punish Cubans who wanted to go to the U.S. People who wanted to leave were only allowed to take about five dollars, one outfit such as a suit or dress, and underwear.

*These Cubans took airplane flights to Key West, Florida, shortly after Castro took over. They arrived in the U.S. on October 15, 1960.*

*These Cubans were at a **refugee** center close to Miami, Florida, in about 1960.*

Castro made many changes in Cuba. High-school students had to leave home and work for the government. Many Cuban parents worried about their children's future. Through a plan known as Operation Pedro Pan, which is Spanish for "Peter Pan," about 14,000 Cuban children came alone to the United States between 1960 and 1962. Many children were reunited with their parents, but some never saw their parents again.

> I never dreamed that I would be separated from my children for seventeen years.
> —Ada Manero Alvaré, who sent her son and daughter to the United States in Operation Pedro Pan

# A New Life in a New Country

In 1960, the United States established the Cuban **Refugee** Emergency Center in Miami to handle the large numbers of Cuban **exiles** who were forced to leave Cuba. Almost all Cubans who came to the United States went through this center. The center gave people a place to stay, doctors to help them, and food to eat. Workers at the center helped Cubans **settle** in Miami and other areas in the United States.

*This photo shows a Cuban refugee center in the United States in January 1966.*

*Many of the Cubans who came to the United States ended up owning their own shops, like this Cuban-American market in Miami's Little Havana.*

Miami was and still is an important center of Cuban-American life. People who had been lawyers, scientists, or business owners in Cuba would take any jobs they could find so they could stay in Miami. They took jobs washing dishes, cleaning rooms, or carrying guests' bags in hotels. They worked hard, and many later owned their own businesses in the United States.

The city of Miami has two official languages, English and Spanish. In **Little Havana,** most people speak Spanish.

# Leaving Cuba from Mariel

More and more people wanted to leave Cuba because of Castro. People who spoke out against Castro were often put in prison. Children of people who disagreed with the government were teased by other students and also by teachers. In 1980, six Cubans broke into Peru's **embassy** in Havana, Cuba. They were unhappy and wanted to leave Cuba. Many other Cubans felt the same way.

*This map shows some of the areas in the United States that Cubans first moved to and where many still live today.*

### Cuban Immigration to the United States

*Many of the boats carrying* Marielitos *to Florida were so crowded that they sank on their way. The U.S.* **Coast Guard** *rescued people on 1,387 sinking boats.*

In response, Castro said that the government would let some people go to the United States. They had to leave by boat from the harbor in the city of Mariel. They also had to find their own way to go to the United States. Many Cuban Americans paid people to go to Cuba to pick up family members and friends. But it was not always clear who was supposed to be on which boat. People got on any boat they could. Often, it was not the boat that was sent for them.

Because the boats left from Mariel, these **immigrants** came to be known as *Marielitos.*

At school, we only had mayonnaise sandwiches. If the teacher found out you were from a family that had had money before, you were the last to get a sandwich.

—Jorge Castillo, who immigrated when he was 21 years old

# The Marielitos Arrive

From April to September of 1980, about 125,000 Cubans came to Florida. They came with nothing more than the clothes they were wearing. The U.S. government had to find places for the new **immigrants** to stay. People who had family or friends in Florida were able to stay with them. Those who did not know anyone in Florida had to stay in **refugee** camps.

One camp was set up at the Orange Bowl, the stadium for the Miami Dolphins football team. Tents were set up on the field. Doctors took care of sick people in the locker rooms.

*These children were among the thousands of Cubans who left Cuba in 1980.*

*The U.S. government, the **Red Cross**, and other organizations provided food and other basic needs to the people who waited in camps.*

About 100,000 Cubans were taken to camps on four **military bases** in Florida, Indiana, Arkansas, and Wisconsin. Sometimes, they had to wait there for as long as a year. They lived in barracks, which are large rooms with many beds. Fidel Castro had put prisoners from Cuban jails onto boats during this time. These **criminals** also lived at the camps, making them dangerous places.

I found some other people who were not criminals and we took turns standing guard. They [the former prisoners] would steal our things when we were sleeping.
—Jorge Castillo, who immigrated in 1980 when he was 21 years old

# Living in the United States

Cuban Americans had always taken care of new Cuban **immigrants** by helping them find jobs and places to live. The *Marielitos,* however, had a difficult time because Castro had forced many **criminals** to go with them. People living in the United States thought most of the

In 1994, U.S. President Bill Clinton decided that only about 12,000 people from Cuba could enter the U.S., even though about 30,000 Cubans tried to enter. Many Cubans still try to enter the U.S. each year.

*Marielitos* were criminals. Over time, this view of the *Marielitos* went away. There were many good, honest, hardworking people who immigrated to the United States from Cuba.

*These people were among thousands of Cubans who tried to reach the U.S. in boats and rafts in 1994.*

*In 1999, five-year-old Elian Gonzales was found off the coast of Florida floating in an inner tube. The boat he and his mother took from Cuba had sank. The U.S. government decided Elian should go back to Cuba where his father lived. This decision upset many people, especially Cuban Americans, who thought he should be able to stay in the U.S.*

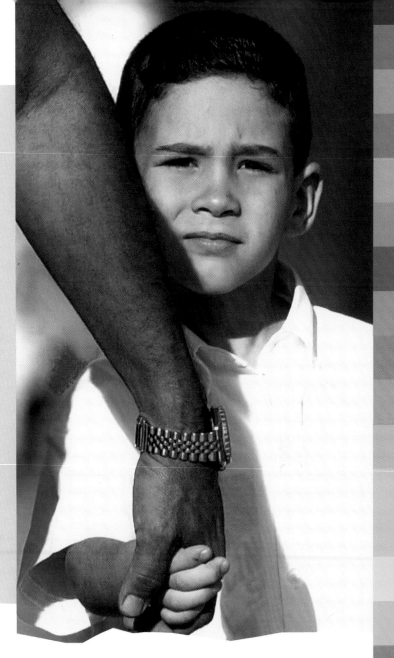

Most Cuban immigrants **settle** in Miami. Miami has a strong Cuban-American community. In an area of Miami known as **Little Havana**, Cuban Americans own shops, restaurants, and other businesses. There are companies that publish books, magazines, and newspapers in Spanish. There are radio and television stations that are in Spanish. There is even a Cuban-American symphony orchestra.

# Families and Work

In most Cuban-American families, grandparents play an important role. Grandparents often take care of children and help around the house. The mother in a **traditional** Cuban family took care of the children and the home while the father went to work. Today, however, many Cuban-American mothers work outside the home, just like Cuban-American men.

*Families like this one enjoy the Cuban American Heritage Festival in Key West, Florida, every summer. It is a celebration of Cuban **culture** in the United States.*

*Roberto Goizueta, shown here, was born in Havana, Cuba. He moved to Miami with little more than a suitcase in 1961 and became the president of Coca-Cola in 1981.*

Cuban Americans have all kinds of jobs. Some own businesses, some are doctors or lawyers, and some work in shops or on farms. In Florida and Louisiana, some Cuban Americans work on farms that grow oranges, tomatoes, and sugarcane. In New York and New Jersey, many Cuban Americans work in factories that make clothes.

José Canseco **immigrated** to the United States from Cuba with his family when he was a baby. He was the first baseball player ever to hit 40 home runs and steal 40 bases in one season.

# Food and Games

In Miami, people can buy some kinds of Cuban foods and drinks that are not available in other areas of the United States. Cuban tamales are ground cornmeal with small chunks of pork wrapped in cornhusks. Cuban Americans sometimes drink *guarapo*. *Guarapo* is a juice made from fresh sugarcane. It seems like juice from sugarcane would be very sweet. But it is only a little sweeter than orange juice.

Drinks that taste like pineapple, watermelon, and coconut are popular in **Little Havana**. Shakes are also popular. Instead of ordering a chocolate shake, though, a Cuban American might get a papaya, mango, or pineapple shake.

*These Cuban Americans ran a booth with Cuban foods at a festival in Miami called Calle Ocho.*

24

*These Cuban-American men are shown playing dominoes in Miami's Little Havana.*

While sipping shakes and *guarapos*, Cuban Americans might be found playing dominoes or *cubilete*. Both games are very popular. *Cubilete* is a **traditional** Cuban game. It is played with five dice. Instead of having one to six dots on each side, these dice have pictures like the 9, 10, Jack, Queen, King, and Ace playing cards. Players try to roll five dice with the same picture. Five aces scores the highest.

# Celebrations and Customs

Cuban Americans have their own **traditions** for celebrating New Year's Eve. During the week before New Year's Day, children build a scarecrow called the *Año Viejo,* which means "old year" in Spanish. They use old clothes and stuff the clothes with paper. At midnight on New Year's Eve, everyone says goodbye to the old year, and the *Año Viejo* is burned. Another Cuban-American New Year's Eve tradition is to eat twelve grapes when midnight strikes. Each grape stands for one month in the new year.

*This Cuban woman lit 2,000 candles on New Year's Eve 1999 in Havana, Cuba.*

*The typical* quinceañera, *or fifteenth birthday party, includes fancy dresses, gifts, and a large feast.*

Another popular Cuban American tradition is to throw a big party for girls when they turn fifteen. In Cuba, fifteen is the traditional age at which a girl can be married. Today it would be very unlikely that a Cuban-American girl would get married at such a young age. Even so, there is a large party like a wedding to celebrate a girl's fifteenth birthday.

Most Cuban Americans are **Roman Catholic.** Each year on September 8, Cuban-American churches have a special event to celebrate the **patron saint of Cuba.** She is called Our Lady of Charity. A statue of the saint is carried through the streets near the church.

# Christopher Bello Today

After eighteen days in the camp in Arkansas, Christopher went to Alameda, California, to live with his father. He learned English at a college that offered classes for Cuban **refugees.** Christopher decided he wanted to be a real estate agent, which is a person who buys, sells, or rents buildings. In 1987, he moved to San Francisco and began working. Soon after, Christopher opened a restaurant that served Cuban food. The restaurant was a success.

*San Francisco's Golden Gate Bridge can be seen in the background of this picture of Christopher.*

I always wanted to be free, but I didn't know what that meant. Freedom comes from within . . . In Cuba, I wasn't able to dream of being free of those things around me. Here, I have hope.

—Christopher Bello

In 1991, Christopher had his mother come to the United States from Cuba. She lived with him for ten years. As she grew older, she needed someone to take care of her all the time. Christopher's sisters in Cuba said they could take care of their mother. His sisters worked with the Cuban government and their mother returned to Cuba. Today, Christopher lives in San Francisco and is a cook there. He loves Cuban **culture.** He also loves being an American who is free to live life the way he wants to.

*Christopher is shown here with his mother, who used to live with him in San Francisco.*

# Cuban Immigration Chart

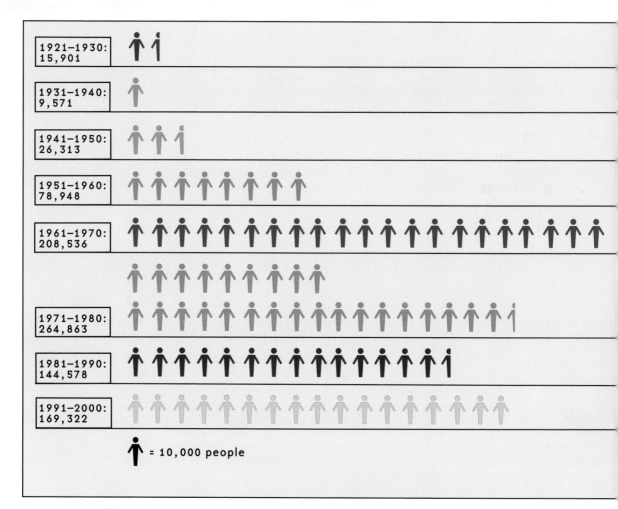

| | |
|---|---|
| 1921–1930: 15,901 | 👤👤 |
| 1931–1940: 9,571 | 👤 |
| 1941–1950: 26,313 | 👤👤 |
| 1951–1960: 78,948 | 👤👤👤👤👤👤👤👤 |
| 1961–1970: 208,536 | 👤👤👤👤👤👤👤👤👤👤👤👤👤👤👤👤👤👤👤👤👤 |
| 1971–1980: 264,863 | 👤👤👤👤👤👤👤👤👤👤👤👤👤👤👤👤👤👤👤👤👤👤👤👤👤👤 |
| 1981–1990: 144,578 | 👤👤👤👤👤👤👤👤👤👤👤👤👤👤 |
| 1991–2000: 169,322 | 👤👤👤👤👤👤👤👤👤👤👤👤👤👤👤👤👤 |

👤 = 10,000 people

*More than 900,000 Cuban people came to the United States from 1921 to 2000.*

Source: U.S. Immigration and Naturalization Service

# More Books to Read

Gernand, Renèe. *The Cuban Americans.* New York: Chelsea House Publishers, 1996.

Hahn, Laura M. *The Cuban Americans.* Philadelphia, Pa.: Mason Crest Publishers, 2003.

Sonneborn, Liz. *The Cuban Americans.* San Diego, Calif.: Lucent Books, 2002.

# Glossary

**climate** typical weather of a place over a number of years

**Coast Guard** branch of the United States military that protects the country's coasts

**colony** territory that is owned or ruled by another country

**communist** person or government that supports communism, a political system in which there is one party and government owns all factories, natural resources, and goods

**criminal** someone who has broken the law

**culture** ideas, skills, arts, and way of life for a certain group of people

**dictator** ruler with complete power over a country

**embassy** country's official office in a foreign country

**exile** person who leaves his or her home country because of political reasons

**guerrilla** member of a small band of armed soldiers formed to fight against a force in charge of a country

**immigrate** to come to a country to live there for a long time. A person who immigrates is an immigrant.

**industry** business

**Little Havana** area of Miami that is the center of Cuban-American culture. It is named for the capital city of Cuba.

**military base** main place for a particular group of soldiers

**natural resource** thing found in nature that people can sell or use, like gold or oil

**patron saint** holy person thought to watch over and help a certain group of people

**Red Cross** voluntary group that works to help people around the world

**refugee** person who has to go away from his or her country and who can't return home because he or she could be hurt

**Roman Catholic** religion led by the pope that follows the teachings of the Bible

**settle** to make a home for yourself and others

**tradition** belief or practice handed down through the years from one generation to the next

# ndex